冬天

Sharing the Planet | Non-Fiction Series

Copyright © 2022 by Level Learning, INC. and Washington Yu Ying PCS™
Original and Edited Text Copyright © 2022 by Washington Yu Ying PCS™

All rights reserved. No part of this book in whole or part may be reproduced without written permission from the publisher.

Published by Level Learning, INC.

Content Contributors:
Washington Yu Ying PCS™
Level Learning - Jingyao Qi

Illustrations by: Josh Taira

Leveling classification based on Level Learning standard. For full description, visit www.levellearning.com

ISBN 978-1-64040-051-1
Simplified Chinese Edition

About Level Learning:
Level Learning provides a literacy focused curriculum specifically designed for K-12 Chinese as a Second Language classrooms. Our program offers 20 levels of specific and detailed objectives, leveled texts and passages, mastery-based online assessment, and analytics to enable data-driven instruction. Level Learning reading curriculum for both literature and informational text emphasize grammar and comprehension skills to help teachers develop confident and independent Chinese language readers. The non-fiction series of books are specifically designed to support our informational text course based on multiple national standards. To learn more about our entire offering, visit www.levellearning.com.

About Washington Yu Ying PCS™:
Washington Yu Ying PCS is a Mandarin English dual language immersion International Baccalaureate (IB) World school. Yu Ying's mission is to inspire and prepare young people to create a better world by challenging them to reach their full potential in a nurturing Chinese/English educational environment. Yu Ying's comprehensive IB, dual immersion curriculum equips students with global competencies for success in the real world. As a leader in immersion education, Yu Ying is determined to advance Chinese language programs and global citizenry education by helping other schools create and strengthen their Chinese programs. For more information, email: products@washingtonyuying.org

冬天来了！冬天来了！

冬天常常下雪。

雪是白色的,树也变白了。

冬天的天气很冷。

小鸟怕冷。小鸟躲在家里。

小狗怕冷。小狗也躲在家里。

小朋友们不怕冷,他们在堆雪人呢!

小雪人是白色的。小雪人有眼睛、鼻子和嘴巴。

小雪人真好看!小朋友们喜欢他们的小雪人。

Glossary

	Pinyin	English Definition
冬天	dōng tiān	winter
常常	cháng cháng	often
雪	xuě	snow
白色	bái sè	white
树	shù	tree
变	biàn	change
天气	tiān qì	weather
冷	lěng	cold
怕	pà	afraid
躲	duǒ	to hide
家里	jiā li	inside the home
堆	duī	to pile or build
雪人	xuě rén	snowman
眼睛	yǎn jing	eyes
鼻子	bí zi	nose
嘴巴	zuǐ ba	mouth

www.ingramcontent.com/pod-product-compliance
Lightning Source LLC
Chambersburg PA
CBHW041222070526
44584CB00001B/51